COYOTE

NORTH AMERICA'S DOG

BY STEPHEN R. SWINBURNE

BOYDS MILLS PRESS
HONESDALE, PENNSYLVANIA

Many thanks to Kim Royar, wildlife biologist for Vermont Fish and
Wildlife Department, for her help in reviewing the manuscript.

Photographs: Stephen R. Swinburne: Pages: 6, 7, 8 (bottom), 29; Franz J.
Camenzind: Pages: 19, 23 (middle,bottom left), 27, 30; National Park Service:
Pages: 1, 3, 4, 5, 8 (top), 9 (left), 10, 11, 12, 13, 14, 15, 16, 17, 18, 20, 21 (top),
23 (top left, bottom right), 24, 25, 26, 31, 32; United States Fish and Wildlife
Service: Page: 21 (bottom); Vermont Fish and Wildlife Department: Page: 9 (right);
Jeff Henry: Page 22.

Boyds Mills Press, Inc.
A Highlights Company
815 Church Street
Honesdale, Pennsylvania 18431
Printed in China
www.boydsmillspress.com

Publisher Cataloging-in-Publication Data
Swinburne, Stephen R.
   Coyote : North America's dog / by Stephen R. Swinburne.—1st ed.
   [32]p. : col. Ill. ;   cm.
Summary: An examination of coyotes, their behavior and habitat.
ISBN 978-1-56397-765-7 (hc)   978-1-59078-485-3 (pb)
1. Coyotes—Juvenile literature.   [1. Coyotes.]   I. Title.
599.77 -dc21   1999   AC   CIP

Library of Congress Catalog Card Number 98-88215

First edition, 1999
The text of this book is set in 13-point Garamond Book.

10 9 8 7 6 (hc)
10 9 8 7 6 5 4 3 2 1 (pb)

CONTENTS

PROLOGUE

ON AN EARLY AUTUMN EVENING, I sit on a hillside listening for coyotes. All I can hear is the stop-and-start chirp of a cricket and the far-off good-night bellow of a cow. Along the edges of the woods, coyotes should be stirring from an afternoon's rest. The half-grown coyote pups will be hungry and ready to begin the night's hunt.

I peer into the gathering darkness, wondering if the coyotes are out there. Are they watching me? Are they nervous, waiting for me to leave? After a long chilly wait, I'm ready to give up on hearing coyotes for the night. But as I stand and start for home, the coyote chorus erupts.

A crazy mixture of yips, yaps, barks, and howls breaks the silence. It's hard to tell if there are three or thirty coyotes or if they are close or a mile away. Surrounded by dark with a field of stars overhead, the coyotes' wild voices take my breath away. I want to join in and lift my face skyward to sing coyote music, too. But the spirited calls last no more than a minute and end in a sudden, clear wail. The night falls silent again. The coyotes are on the prowl.

As a naturalist, I've learned that coyotes call to communicate with other coyotes. Like wolves, coyotes use their howls to locate other pack members, to tell others a territory is occupied, and to greet members that were separated from the pack. While coyotes often call around sunset and sunrise, you can hear them at any time of day and at any time of year. Two coyotes may sound like a pack of ten because coyotes can quickly change octaves while calling, giving the impression that a lot more animals are present. Coyotes make more kinds of calls than any other animal in North America.

Coyotes fascinate me. I can't think of another creature whose intelligence and cunning allow it to adapt and thrive in nearly every habitat. From the forests of Canada to the deserts of Mexico, coyotes survive.

Not everyone in North America likes coyotes. Because some coyotes prey on livestock, many farmers and ranchers view them as pests. For over one hundred years coyotes have been the most persecuted and most misunderstood predator in North America.

I've watched coyotes in the desert country of the Grand Canyon. I've heard them howl from the hills of Los Angeles. After studying their fascinating behavior, I wonder if it's time to set aside our old prejudices. Will we continue to see the coyote as a symbol of savagery and greed? Or can we learn to get along with this remarkable wild creature and come to appreciate its place in the natural world?

CHAPTER ONE

COYOTES AND THE FARMER

Jon Wright's ruddy face and big callused hands say a lot about this hard-working first-generation farmer before you ever speak to him. Jon and his wife, Kate, run a dairy farm about five miles from where I live in southern Vermont. On an early December morning, Jon (on the left in the photograph) and I walk through a cow pasture a quarter of a mile from his barn. Jon tells me about his coyote experiences.

"We hear coyotes nearly every night in the summer," Jon says. "They really get going about two in the morning."

I ask him how he feels about having coyotes on the farm.

"They've been around New England longer than I have, so I guess they have as much right to be here as we do," says Jon. "Although I don't hunt them and wouldn't

shoot one, we run the farm knowing that coyotes are out there. I sort of see them as an occupational hazard." Jon shows me a field where he hays. "I often see coyotes trailing me when I'm haying," Jon says. "They pick up mice and snakes that I've run over with the tractor."

Jon is no dyed-in-the-wool predator lover. He knows what coyotes can do. "We lost a calf this summer to a pack of coyotes. A heifer calved in a field, then walked back to the barn, leaving the calf out all night," Jon says. "I ask myself if we might have saved the calf if I'd kept the cow closer to the barn. We're learning to live with coyotes, knowing what we can and can't do."

Some people who raise sheep have discovered that keeping guard dogs is an effective way to cope with coyotes. The practice of using large dogs to protect sheep started in Europe long ago. Certain kinds of dogs, such as the Eurasian breed called Akbash, will bond with sheep

Coyotes stay clear of sheep protected by llamas.

when released into the flock at an early age. As the dogs grow up, they become the flock's leader. Then the dogs protect the flock from predators. Llamas and donkeys are also protective and will bond with sheep. Many sheep herders who keep llamas notice fewer losses to coyotes.

Jon Wright may tolerate the presence of a predator on his property. But to many ranchers and farmers, the only good coyote is a dead coyote. Some coyotes get an appetite for livestock and occasionally kill sheep, young cows, and chickens.

Livestock damages are greatest in many western states where ranchers keep huge herds of sheep. Since the late

1800s, ranchers and farmers have sought protection for their livestock. At the turn of the twentieth century, the United States Government began destroying predators throughout the country. Although the use of poison as a predator control was outlawed in 1972, it is still legal in certain states to kill coyotes at any time of the year if you have a hunting license. Some states allow hunting and trapping coyotes for their fur from November to February.

In Massachusetts a recent law made the use of foot-hold traps illegal. Most biologists agree that individual coyotes that prey on livestock and poultry should be destroyed. But scientists also firmly believe that not all coyotes are troublemakers. They have a rightful place in nature

Pictures from the U.S. Government's program to eliminate predators from Yellowstone National Park: soldiers pose with a dead wolf in the summer of 1905; a coyote captured in a foot-hold trap around 1929.

Coyotes scavenge on the carcass of an elk during a winter in Yellowstone.

because they help preserve the ecological balance. Up to 80 percent of their diet consists of destructive rodents such as voles, rats, and mice.

Just like the family dog, coyotes spend a lot of time looking for something to eat. They will eat anything they can chew, from mice to moose to mulberries. That makes them omnivores and is one of the reasons coyotes are so successful. They adapt, or adjust, to many environments. While great at "mousing," they'll also eat whatever is on the menu: squirrel, gopher, woodchuck, rabbit, deer, elk, bison, moose, house cat, porcupine, opossum, lizard, roadrunner, goose, duck, prickly pear cactus, apples, watermelons, figs, corn, insects, fish, frogs, snakes, pine nuts, acorns, blueberries, road kills, cow carcasses, and garbage.

Bob Crabtree, one of the leading coyote experts in the United States, calls the coyote "the most effective large predator in America." Three things make the coyote an amazing hunter: a keen sense of smell, excellent hearing, and acute vision. Coyotes can smell food and enemies more than a mile away. They can also hear and see small movements of a mouse in tall grass from across a field. Unlike cats, which wait and ambush their prey, coyotes, like other members of the dog family (wolves, jackals, foxes), depend on speed and run down their prey.

NATURE DICTIONARY

Ecology: *the study of animals and plants in their environments.*

Ecosystem: *a community where animals and plants live and produce.*

Habitat: *the natural environment of a plant or animal that provides food, water, shelter, and space for it to survive.*

Range: *an area where an animal or plant is found.*

Weaned: *when a young animal switches from mother's milk to solid food.*

CHAPTER TWO

COYOTE, THE TRICKSTER

FOR OVER TEN THOUSAND YEARS, THE COYOTE has played a large part in Native American culture. Stories are told about the mischievous and wise "little wolf." The Sioux know the coyote as "Iktome," the singing trickster. The Crow view the coyote as a supernatural being and call him Old Man Coyote. The Blackfoot Indians say, "Whoever shall fire upon a coyote or wolf, their barrel will never shoot straight again." Southwestern desert tribes call him God's dog. Native Americans celebrate coyotes for their intelligence and adaptability. One legend says that "if all the creatures in the world were to die, the coyote would be the last one left."

Some Native Americans believe that the coyote has special powers. Legends have been handed down from generation to generation. The coyote comes in three forms: the Creator, the Transformer, and the Trickster, depending on the tribe. As Creator, some tribes believe Coyote made the first people from feathers and mud and gave the people food. Some tribes believe Coyote was the Transformer, endowed with powers to move mountains and change the heavens. Many tribes know Coyote as the Trickster, a mischief-maker and a cheat. A Trickster tale from the Kalispel tribe of Idaho shows how the coyote is always trying to outsmart others but ends up looking silly and foolish:

Once upon a time someone stole the moon. When the people got tired of the dark nights, they looked for someone to be the moon.

"I will do it," said Yellow Fox. But when they put him in the sky, he shone so brightly that he made things hot at night. So they had to take him down.

Then the people went to Coyote. They asked him, "Would you like to be the moon?"

"I sure would," Coyote said. He smiled because he knew that as the moon he could see everything on earth. They placed Coyote in the sky. He did not make the nights too hot and bright. For a time the people were pleased.

Coyote

Wolf

COYOTE FACTS

Some people mistake coyotes for wolves. Although they look alike, wolves can be three times heavier than coyotes. The average weight of a coyote is about forty pounds.

Coyotes and wolves belong in the Canid, or dog, family, which includes jackals, dingoes, foxes, and domestic dogs. While biologists believe wolves originated in the world's boreal and Arctic regions, coyotes are native to North America.

European settlers called the coyote "brush wolf" or "prairie wolf," but the coyote is America's true dog. The coyote's Latin name is Canis latrans, *meaning "barking dog."*

"Coyote is doing a good job as the moon," they agreed.

But Coyote, the moon, could see everything. He could see people doing wrong and he would shout down, "Hey, that man is stealing meat from the drying racks" or "That person is cheating at the moccasin game."

Finally, all the people who wished to do things in secret got together. "Take Coyote out of the sky," they said. "He is making too much noise with all his shouting."

So Coyote was taken out of the sky. Someone else became the moon. Coyote could no longer see what everyone on earth was doing, but that hasn't stopped him from still trying to snoop into everyone else's business ever since.

CHAPTER THREE

WATCHING YELLOWSTONE COYOTES

IT'S A COLD FEBRUARY MORNING, and I'm standing on a frozen, wild stretch of road in the Lamar Valley of Yellowstone National Park. Through my binoculars I watch a coyote hunt his breakfast. Fifty feet from the edge of the road, the coyote tiptoes through a fresh blanket of white. Head low, its yellow eyes burn into the snow. The coyote's ears are pricked, listening for the squeaks and scurrying of a mouse tunneling under eight inches of snow.

The coyote freezes in its tracks, every sense focused on one spot. It springs three feet in the air, eyes still glued to the invisible target below. It pounces on the spot and

COYOTE FACTS

Coyotes form packs like wolves, but they are not as long-term or as large. Four or five coyotes come together in the spring to help raise the young pups.

The parents are the alpha pair or lead members of the pack, and they, along with other pack members, gather food and baby-sit young. At a kill, the young wait until the parents eat.

Pups usually leave the pack around six months of age. Unpaired adult coyotes may go through the winter as loners.

lands forefeet first, pinning its prey. The coyote's head disappears and then lifts with a snout full of snow and a mouth full of mouse. I watch the coyote take two quick bites and swallow. The coyote looks up at me and then continues hunting. Three times the coyote performs this mousing ballet. Researchers say that when hunting, coyotes can usually catch small prey such as mice and voles about every twenty minutes.

An hour of walking this wind-blown tarmac has turned my hands and face numb. I think about the heat in my parked car. Before I go, I take a last look. While I wouldn't last long in this brutally cold environment, the coyote seems perfectly adapted. Its long, insulating fur keeps the coyote warm. Its sharp teeth and awesome speed keep it well fed. Through my binoculars I see the coyote point its

Wolves howling. Most coyotes are killed by wolves when caught scavenging at elk carcasses.

nose, sniffing the wind, every sense alert for the presence of food or the possibility of danger.

Yellowstone coyotes have had something new to worry about over the last few years. In 1995 and 1996, the U.S. Fish and Wildlife Service reintroduced gray wolves from Canada into Yellowstone National Park. Biologists believe there are about one hundred wolves in the park. Wolves compete with coyotes for territory and food. Gray wolves outweigh their rivals and will kill them on the spot if they discover them.

The coyote I watched in the Lamar Valley of Yellowstone might be part of the long-term study on coyotes conducted by Dr. Bob Crabtree, chief coyote biologist in Yellowstone. Crabtree began his research in the park in 1989. Since wolves were returned to Yellowstone in 1995, Crabtree has focused on wolf-coyote competition and what reduced

In the winter of 1995, eight wolves were released into Yellowstone, the first to roam free since 1926.

numbers of coyotes mean for Yellowstone's ecology. He estimates that since wolves were first released more than 150 coyotes have been killed.

Bob Crabtree and his team of researchers hope to answer some fascinating questions about coyotes in the Yellowstone ecosystem. Will coyotes have to change their territories, their social structure, or their diet in order to survive the pressures of the growing wolf population? Will coyotes be driven from Yellowstone entirely? Crabtree doesn't think so. He says coyotes will always survive, but at lower numbers, probably similar to the early 1900s, when wolves were common in Yellowstone. Wildlife biologists

COYOTE FACTS

Dr. Bob Crabtree, seen here among part of Yellowstone's bison herd, estimates that wolves kill about 20 percent of Yellowstone's coyote population each winter.

Male and female coyotes mate for life, or until one animal dies. The oldest coyote on record was a sixteen-year-old coyote from Colorado. Most coyotes live about five to seven years.

Like wolves, coyotes give birth to their pups in dens. Average litters are four to eight pups. Coyotes often make a number of suitable dens in their territory.

Adults will move pups from den to den to avoid predators. Adults closely guard their young. A male will do all the hunting when pups are first born, bringing food to his mate.

When pups are weaned, they feed on partially digested meat that the adults regurgitate. At twelve weeks, pups leave the den and travel with their parents.

continue to study the competition between coyote and wolf, eager to learn how the story unfolds.

In most places in the United States coyote is top dog with few enemies. In certain national parks and wilderness areas, mountain lions and wolves kill coyotes. Thousands of coyotes are killed by cars every year throughout North America.

A few years after watching that lone coyote hunt his winter breakfast, I return to Yellowstone National Park in the summer to see firsthand wolf-coyote interaction. At twilight, on a midsummer's day, I stand with other wolf watchers in the Lamar Valley in the northern part of Yellowstone Park. This spot has become one of the best places in the United States to observe wild wolves in their natural environment and also to see wolves and coyotes interact.

Thousands come to Yellowstone each year to watch wolves, coyotes, and other wildlife.

Just before the last light, someone in our group, with eyes glued to the rim of her field glasses, calls, "Wolves!" Binoculars rise and focus on five members of the Druid Peak wolf pack crossing a brush-covered ridge a half-mile away. Outlined against a reddening sky, a small band of elk beat a hasty retreat.

In the last moments of light, we can barely make out two coyotes fleeing from the wolves. A silver sliver of moon hangs in a corner of sky and frantic yips from the coyotes tell us that somewhere out of sight wolves are beating up their coyote brethren.

A coyote carries on the never-ending search for food in the Yellowstone winter.

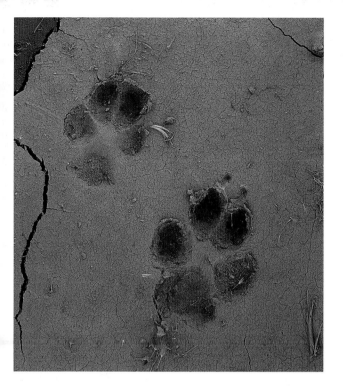

CHAPTER FOUR

ON THE TRACKS OF THE COYOTE

WHEN EUROPEANS FIRST ARRIVED IN NORTH AMERICA, coyotes were strictly a western species. Their range extended from southern Alberta, Canada, to central Mexico and from the Mississippi River west to Arizona, Nevada, Idaho, and Montana. By the early 1900s, coyotes began expanding their range, spreading in every direction. Biologists believed this range expansion was due to the war on wolves during the 1800s and early 1900s. As wolves were destroyed to make way for human settlements and cattle ranching, wolf habitats became vacant. Coyotes moved in to take the wolf's place.

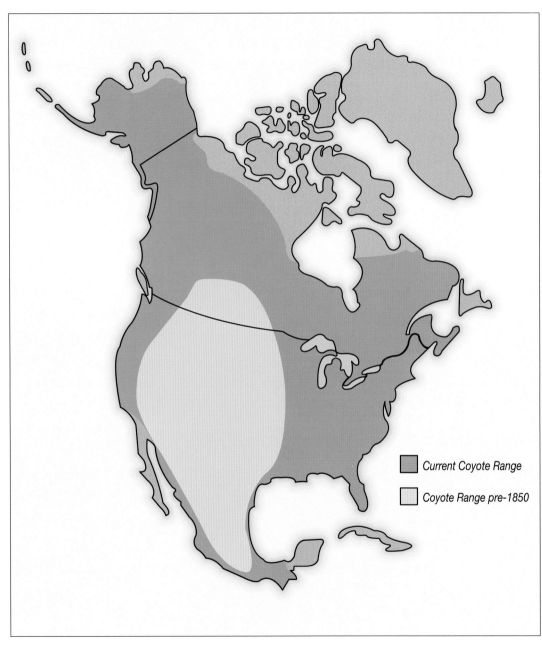

Current Coyote Range

Coyote Range pre-1850

COYOTE FACTS

What is a "coydog?" A coydog is a hybrid, the result of a wild coyote and a domestic or feral dog mating.

Most wildlife biologists believe coydog populations cannot get established because of two important reasons: coyote-dog hybrids give birth to pups in the middle of the winter, a hard time to gather food for a litter of pups, and male coyote-dog hybrids do not help raise and protect the pups.

Coyotes are wild animals and do not make good pets. As with all wild animals, it is best to show respect and never approach too close.

Some coyotes migrated north and east, and along the way bred with a smaller race of Canadian timber wolf. The result of the western coyote-wolf cross is a larger and darker eastern coyote, more like a German shepherd. Records show that this new kind of coyote arrived in Minnesota in 1875 and Pennsylvania in 1907. During the 1920s, coyotes migrated to Ontario and Quebec. By the 1930s, eastern coyotes had reached New York. Coyotes arrived in Massachusetts in 1940, New Hampshire in 1944, and Vermont in 1948. By 1970, coyotes inhabited every state but Hawaii. Now coyotes live everywhere from Alaska and most of Canada to as far south as Costa Rica and Panama, from Maine to the tip of Baja California and every place in between.

One early October morning on a sandbar along a lonely stretch of the West River in South Londonderry, Vermont, I find a set of coyote tracks at the river's edge.

One October morning I tracked a coyote along a sandy stretch of a Vermont river.

I follow them and try to figure out what the coyote was doing. The tracks run in a straight line, never straying left or right, as if the coyote was on a mission. The coyote prints cross a narrow wash, and I lose them for a moment.

On hands and knees, I stare intently at the mud and stones, trying to read the messages written in the riverbank. I begin thinking about that coyote. What a successful newcomer it is to these woods. All across the country—in woodlands, meadows, and towns—sooner or later people will one day see or hear this new predator. Most wildlife biologists believe the coyote population in the United States is on the increase.

On the other side of the wash, I pick up the coyote's tracks. Why did the coyote come this way? Was it hoping to find a dead trout or an unsuspecting frog along the riverbank? Did it pause to sip from the stream? I feel like a wildlife detective trying to solve the case of the elusive coyote. All the clues are here. It's up to me to figure out the puzzle.

Whatever first attracted the coyote to the waterside eventually lost the animal's interest. The tracks veer away from the water and enter a narrow swath of river grass, where I lose them in a tangle of alder and willow trees. I stand searching the spaces between the trees, hoping to see the coyote of my tracks looking back at me. But these are the coyote's woods. He knows them better than I do. He is a master of adaptability. He is a survivor.

Wherever the coyote steps is home.

COYOTE FACTS

If you're reading this somewhere in North America, chances are good that you're closer to coyotes than you think. Coyotes are highly intelligent, extremely adaptable, and very secretive animals.

They have even learned to live in cities. Biologists believe that about five thousand coyotes live in Los Angeles. Coyotes were seen in the Bronx, New York, for the first time in the early 1990s.

And how are coyotes surviving as city dwellers? Just fine—eating rats, cats, and garbage, and denning in waste lots, culverts, and tunnels.

A coyote in Hollywood, California.

INDEX